Introduction

This resource seeks to provide practical examples, for use and adaptation, of strategies and materials to help teachers develop further the assessment practice within RE in their school. Examples of approaches related to specific religions are drawn on, as well as providing opportunities to address the pupils' own world views and ideas. Each section is illustrative and can be adapted to meet the learning outcomes and assessment opportunities provided by the individual school's scheme of work.

Assessment in RE is for many a difficult and even sometimes contentious issue. Evidence from Ofsted, Estyn and others suggests that overall assessment in RE, whilst it has improved in recent years, is less developed or effective than in some other subject areas. RE teachers face particular issues, not least in terms of the numbers of classes and pupils they are responsible for in any given week. This resource seeks to take these issues into consideration and make a practical contribution to help teachers develop more effective practice in RE assessment.

Different curriculum arrangements for RE in different parts of the United Kingdom means that there are slightly different emphases and approaches towards levels of attainment. We have drawn on the non-statutory levels of the English Qualification and Curriculum Authority's (QCA's) framework for RE whilst taking into consideration guidance from others. Some of the wording and terminology differs in the four partner nations, but the aim of high quality teaching and learning experiences leading to high standards in RE in which assessment plays a vital part is common.

Pamela Draycott
Series Editor

Contents

- 2 RE and Assessment – Frequently Asked Questions (FAQs)
- 4 Marking Pupils' Work: An Effective Shortcut
- 8 Using Assessment Criteria to Boost Attainment
- 12 Teachings of Jesus: The Parable of the Sheep and the Goats
- 16 Learning from Sikhism: Using a Question Bank
- 20 Assessing Skills and Viewpoints: Beliefs about God
- 24 Learning and Assessment: Islam and the Idea of God
- 28 'More or Less' Task Setting
- 30 Peer and Self-Assessment in RE

RE and Assessment - FAQ

1. What is assessment?

Assessment is essentially to do with making judgements about pupils' attainment and achievements. The standards against which pupils' achievements in RE are judged are set by the locally agreed syllabus, faith community guidelines or equivalent.

It is important to distinguish between:

- **Assessment** *of* **learning** – this is summative in nature and takes place periodically e.g. an end of unit test. The results are often reported in grades, marks or levels and can be tracked over time; and

- **Assessment** *for* **learning** – this is formative in nature and takes place all the time in the classroom. It is about using the information gained to improve learning. Where expectations and targets are shared with pupils, it can contribute to Assessment *of* learning.

It is important to distinguish between **attainment** (which is peer/age referenced) against some external criteria (such as an eight-level scale) and **achievement** (which is personally referenced) and linked to the individual's capabilities and development.

2. How does assessment promote effective learning?

Assessment promotes effective learning where it:

- is **embedded** in a view of teaching and learning of which it is an integral part;
- involves **sharing learning goals** with pupils;
- aims to help pupils **know and recognise the standards** they are aiming for;
- involves pupils in **self-assessment**;
- provides **feedback** which leads to pupils recognising their next steps in learning and how to tackle them;
- is underpinned by confidence that **every pupil can improve**;
- involves both teacher and pupils **reviewing and reflecting** on assessment data.

3. How important is planning?

Planning is the key to effective assessment. A good RE department will plan to:

- **develop a subject policy** on assessment, drawing on the school's overall policy;

- **set clear, focused objectives** for lessons and **learning outcomes** for tasks which guide the choice of content and activities and help identify whether or not pupils have achieved the goal;

- **use the evidence from assessment** to focus teaching more closely on the individual needs of pupils;

- **set subject-specific targets** once a term at the most, giving pupils the opportunity to improve the identified area of their work over a period of time. Helpful targets are directly related to the RE learning objectives and specify what pupils need to do and how to do it;

- **provide pupil-friendly versions of the level/grade descriptions** and encourage pupils to use them to assess their own and other pupils' work, set targets for improvement and discuss the reasons for their judgement;

- **provide detailed mark schemes** for each major assessment, which put into context the level descriptions to the specific task and discuss with pupils how each level/grade might be achieved.

4. How can information be gained about pupils' learning?

QCA gives the following guidance:

- **observing** pupils as they work and interact with their peers and adults;
- **listening** to pupils as they describe their work and reasoning to others;
- **questioning**, especially the use of open questions which allow for a range of responses;
- **setting** tasks which require the planned use of specific skills;
- **using** a variety of forms of communication e.g. drawing, artefacts, actions, role play, as well as short and extended writing;
- **discussing** words, images, ideas and concepts.

5. How can assessment be made manageable?

The large number of pupils taught by many RE teachers can make meaningful assessment seem daunting! According to Ofsted, the most effective RE departments:

- **ensure that assessment is fully integrated** into curriculum planning and teaching rather than being seen as an 'add on' that requires additional time;
- **develop an RE assessment policy** which interprets the school policy in the light of subject-related issues, such as the relatively short pupil–teacher contact time, e.g. they seek to modify whole-school requirements that cannot be met by the RE department, such as marking every pupil's work weekly;
- **develop systems for 'staggering' or 'sampling' marking** to overcome the problems caused by the large numbers of pupils taught. Pupils' self-assessment and paired assessment can provide valuable feedback. These strategies are most effective where they have the understanding and support of senior management.

6. Is it worth it?

Yes! Many studies show that innovations which include strengthening the practice of formative assessment produces significant and often substantial learning gains. Many also show that improved formative assessment helps lower attainers more than others and so reduces the spread of attainment whilst also raising it overall.

7. Where can I find out more?

A first and crucial reference point is the statutory locally agreed syllabus, faith community, or equivalent. Also, any non-statutory guidelines published by the SACRE.

The information provided here draws significantly on the following:

- *Assessment for Learning*, DfES Ref: 0043-2004G, available for download from www.standards.dfes.gov.uk;
- *Good Assessment Practice in religious education*, HMI 1480 (2003), available for download from www.ofsted.gov.uk
- *Guidance on Assessing RE*, QCA non-statutory guidance on RE (1999).

See also:

- Information on **curriculum balance, assessment** and **religious and moral education** for Scotland, available as three separate downloads from www.ltscotland.org.uk/5to14/guidelines/index.asp

Marking Pupils' RE Work: An Effective Shortcut

For the teacher

Teachers of RE may see 500 pupils a week, but pages of red ticks interspersed with the occasional 'well done' or 'see me' do not inspire pupils to improve. This section suggests a key to making assessment more manageable and meaningful. Assessment needs to provide a useful record of progress and a way of setting direction for future improvement – setting a target. For assessment to be productive it needs actively to engage pupils: after all, it's their work and their brain!

Marking after midnight: a common way for teachers to waste time

What is a comment decoder? Can it make marking twice as useful in half the time?

- This idea gives a clear focus to 'marking' and makes it both communicative and productive.

- The decoder on page 5 can cut your marking time in half while doubling your communication with pupils.

- Assessment for learning theory and research shows very clearly that comment-only marking which sets clear targets raises standards. But writing 500 comments takes a long time.

- Use a decoder to communicate the 26 most common messages you want pupils to receive, in the simplest possible way.

- Have a copy of your decoder for pupils to stick into the front of their books or folders. They will refer to it. Give your assessment of work using three (or more) letters. Ask pupils to match these with comments when their work is returned. They'll enjoy looking up the meaning of BOX, DAG or YUK! Record the letters in your mark book for your own reference.

- In the example on page 5, letters A–N credit attainment using the non-statutory eight-level scale, and set targets for improvement. The 'level' column on the right can be deleted in your pupils' version: focus on the comment, not the number. Letters O–S refer to general study skills and T–Z are praise comments: aim to use at least one of these every time work is marked, in combination with other letters.

 The decoder is available for download by subscribers at www.REToday.org.uk

Create your own comment decoder

Why not try adapting the example from page 5 to make your own decoder? Pupils could suggest comments they find most helpful, encouraging or challenging. Or perhaps your whole school assessment policy requires the letter A–E to be used with set meanings. Fine: use letters F–Z for other meaningful and common comments. The example given concentrates on levels 4–6, but it is not difficult to make your own decoder for lower – or higher – achieving pupils. Linking comments to levels helps recording and target setting, making assessment formative as well as summative. Pupils could have a go at some self- or peer-assessment using this decoder too.

Religious Education comment decoder

Write the meanings of the letters your teacher gives you into the book / folder yourself.

A	You've described the religious materials well. Your target: Try to explain for yourself next time.	4
B	You've given some examples from the religion. Your target: Try to say why the ideas matter to believers next time.	4
C	You've thought about religious meanings here. Next time, try to link up the ideas, the beliefs and what believers do.	4
D	You've given your views about a religious question. Next time, refer to other people's views as well, and say what you think of them.	4
E	You've described some religious ideas well. Next, show how much you understand about the religion – use the right words.	4
F	Your target: Explain clearly how different religious groups are similar.	5
G	Your target: Explain clearly the impact of religion on people's lives.	5
H	Your target: Explain clearly three or more different ways belief is expressed.	5
I	Your target: When you give your own ideas, say how they are similar to / different from the religious ideas you have studied.	5
J	Your target: Express your own views using religious language properly. Comment thoughtfully on other people's ideas.	5
K	Your target: Give your own interpretation of the questions we've looked at, explaining both religious ideas and your own ideas.	6
L	Your target: Use the correct religious words to argue for your own viewpoint, referring to other views clearly.	6
M	Your target: Give your response to inspiring people you study, connecting their lives to your own experience and ideas.	6
N	Your target: Think about the religious and spiritual questions until you have some insight of your own. Express the insight clearly!	6
O	Your target: To finish your work at home and bring it in next time.	S
P	Your target: To finish off each piece of your work.	S
Q	Your target: To write in your own words. Stop copying other people's ideas and answers.	S
R	You've done well at giving your own views. Next you need to include more explanation of religious views.	S
S	See me. I want to talk to you this lesson.	S
T	Your spoken answers are very good. Discussion is your strength.	P
U	This shows you can feel how others feel – good empathy.	P
V	This is real RE – thank you for writing it.	P
W	You've described the religious materials well. Your target: Try to explain for yourself next time.	P
X	Your work made me smile. Good.	P
Y	Good thinking. Keep asking the questions	P
Z	I'm really impressed with your ideas. Keep them coming.	P

What can they do? A baseline assessment strategy for RE

For the teacher

It is important to establish what pupils know, understand and are able to do when they begin their time in your school: then you can more easily target work to their needs, help them to make progress, and set high standards. Much baseline testing is focused on what pupils know (or don't). Provided here is a basic bank of 8 key questions to enable pupils to apply, rather than merely recount, their previous RE learning. Allow pupils a choice in the question(s) they answer (5 might be a maximum). Use this strategy in term 1 of the first year in the school and again in the final term two years higher up the school (Year 7 and Year 9 in most English secondary schools). Keep the earlier work for pupils to compare it with their later work. The work focuses on the experiences of discussion.

Links:

Use discussion and thinking skills strategies to develop pupils' knowledge and confidence in handling these questions, and refer to the PCfRE database of pupils' writing on spiritual and religious questions. Pupils could search this database in class, in ICT lessons or for homework: www.pcfre.org.uk/db

The example (right) shows a pupil who is able to work at level 5, explaining diverse beliefs and ideas about questions of meaning and truth.

How do we know what is right, good or true?

When we are younger we are taught the basics of this by our parents - some people use the Bible for this - Although I think the basic idea of the 10 commandments I don't, personally, look to the Bible for guidance - I think many ideas of what is right, good, & true in the Bible are very out-dated - eg. the idea only men can only marry women, that women are worth less than men etc. I do think some of the Bibles ideas are worth listening to but I don't hold have the view that everything Bible said says is correct.

What is the purpose of dying?

I'm not sure why we die - I know, or at least I hope, it is so we can go on to the next life - Its hard to believe this sometimes in the world we live in but I think I do - It seems unfair when people die before their time but there is nothing we can do to stop it - I wouldn't like to live forever though - I think the more you believe in an after-life, the less scared you are of dying - but I'm not sure - I don't think there is a purpose of dying - only a purpose of living & dying is just the process that takes us on to the next life -

Marking Pupils' RE Work: An Effective Shortcut

Instructions for pupils:

This RE assessment asks about your own views and how well you can express them. Use this sheet to make some simple bullet pointed notes, and then choose the questions (up to five) that interest you most. Discuss the questions with others in the class – and some adults as well if you can – and then write up to five paragraphs that explain your own views and ideas in depth and detail.

Eight key religious and spiritual questions:

1. Religions try to show people the best way to live. When you think about it carefully, what would you say is the best way to live and why?

2. 'Sometimes I get a feeling that I am aware of a presence or power different from my everyday self'. More than a third of people agree with this. Have you ever felt this? Please describe your experience.

3. Some people pray many times a day, others not at all. What are your thoughts about the subject of prayer?

4. In RE, you get chances to learn about religions, think about your own experience and form your own views on life and faith. Please tell us: what do you like about RE?

5. Two viewpoints about death: 'When we die, we lie in the grave, that's it', 'Dying is like being born: you leave a place you know and go to a wonderful place you don't know'. What do you think about death and the afterlife?

6. A big religious question is 'What is God like?' What are your own thoughts and beliefs about God?

7. Religion gives followers a 'vision' or 'hope for the future'. What are your hopes for the future? What sort of world do you dream of?

8. Important ideas in religions are those of freedom, truth, justice, love and forgiveness. What do you think about any three of these concepts?

© 2006 RE Today Services
Permission is granted to photocopy this page for use in classroom activities in schools that have purchased this publication.

Engaging with secondary RE: Assessed RE

Using Assessment Criteria to Boost Attainment

For the teacher
Good practice in **assessment for learning** suggests that teachers and pupils achieve more if:
- questions and tasks are carefully prepared;
- 'I can ...' statements are shared in understandable ways;
- drafting and redrafting is combined with peer review, and;
- pupils can choose their own path through assessment tasks.

All these points can be incorporated in the examples of tasks and assessment approaches outlined here.

Start the cycle of development with the **levels** you are aiming at with your pupils. Add **content** from religions to the levels to set **objectives**.

Take the **objectives** for a lesson or unit of work and use the most **stimulating teaching activity** you have to **build an assessment task**.

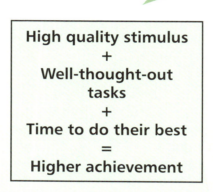

High quality stimulus
+
Well-thought-out tasks
+
Time to do their best
=
Higher achievement

Share the **'I can...'s** with pupils and use them to set the **'next level' challenge**. Review and improve the clarity in the light of pupil understanding.

Use the **skill words** of the levels to create classroom **'I can...' statements**. Show pupils what you're looking for. Revise for simplicity – but don't 'dumb down'.

For the teacher
An eight-level scale, such as those provided by QCA, Agreed Syllabuses or ACCAC, is a good tool for standards and assessment in RE, but needs translating twice. Firstly to put it into the **content-specific language of teachers' planning**. Secondly to make it simple – but not simplistic – language to share with pupils in order to help them clarify their understanding of what is expected in RE. The planning model above shows the cycle of development that this requires of the teacher.

As an example, the QCA scale asks pupils at level 4 to: **'use a developing religious vocabulary to describe and show understanding of (religious) sources and beliefs'**.

Working on the Apostles' Creed and the Mool Mantar, a teacher sets the lesson objective: **'to enable pupils to describe Christian and Sikh beliefs from textual sources and to compare them simply'**.

The pupils are given work to do that leads to these outcomes:

I can...
- describe three things that Christians and Sikhs believe;
- use different texts as sources to identify two beliefs Sikhs and Christians share;
- *show my understanding by suggesting two answers to the question 'Do Sikhs and Christians believe in the same God?'*

Assessment activity 1
'I can...' toolkit for assessing RE – Jewish festivals

	Learning about Judaism I can ...	Learning from Judaism I can ...
Level 3	• describe what happens in a Jewish home at Shabbat; • describe the food on the table for Pesach, and say what it symbolises; • state two ways Shabbat is like Pesach, and two ways in which they are different.	• ask some interesting questions about Jewish festivals; • make a link between Jewish celebrations and the big days in my own life; • make a link between what Jews remember at Pesach and what I remember at New Year.
Level 4	• describe the impact of celebrating Yom Kippur on young Jewish people; • show that I understand why festivals and holy days matter to Jewish people; • use the right words to describe each festival.	• suggest answers to some spiritual questions about celebrations; • apply ideas like festival, remembrance or commitment to the celebrations I take part in.
Level 5	• explain the role of celebrating Shabbat and Pesach in passing the Jewish faith on from one generation to the next; • explain how Jewish festivals are similar to and different from those of another religion.	• express my view of what's good about the family festivals of the Jews; • relate the rituals of Jewish life to my own life and the things I do repeatedly; • explain what influences me and what influences Jewish young people with regard to celebration.
Level 6	• use biblical text and modern practice to interpret some themes of Pesach: e.g. freedom, thankfulness, sacrifice; • explain some reasons why Jewish minority communities may especially value Shabbat.	• express an insight into the meaning of the liberation of the Jews at Exodus for Jewish people today; • consider the challenges to liberate that our society faces, and express my insights into the values of freedom.

These 'I can...' statements put the levels into accessible content-specific 'pupil speak'. Progression from level 3 to 6 might be four years of good progress. The increasing challenge is illustrated with reference to the skills expected of pupils in the 11–14 age range, and with reference to celebrating Shabbat and Pesach. The teacher's judgement about 'best fit' of work to levels is central to the assessment process – www.ncaction.gov.uk includes over 80 pieces of assessed work to help you develop your skills in this area. (Note: the layout of the 'I can ...' statements is different on page 11 – choose a format that suits you and your pupils.)

Assessment activity 2:
Learning from Buddhism – using a question bank

Learning from religion can be well facilitated by sharp questions at the end of a unit. On page 10 there is a **question bank** to prompt pupils to express what they have learned from their work on Buddhism. These can be adapted to suit your programme of study as they are essentially flexible, majoring on pupil's own ideas and insights. Ask pupils to pick any four and write 50–75 words in response to each. You could tweak the questions to focus more specifically on the content you taught and the abilities of your pupils. The activity is self-differentiating, and can produce evidence of levels 4–7 of the English QCA expectations. It provides a good structure for open-ended work with more able (gifted and talented) pupils. Set it, for example, after discussion, as a 'books open' homework task. To simplify this task for lower-achieving pupils, ask them to do three from eight, using the simpler questions. Higher achieving pupils may need to be directed to some of the more challenging questions.

 To ease adaptation a pdf and Word document of page 10 is available for subscribers to download from www.retoday.org.uk

Choose any from these 16 questions and write 50–75 words in response to each one

1. What do you think are the best things about being a young Buddhist in Britain today?

2. What similarities and differences between the Buddha and another inspiring human being can you see? Explain your choices.

3. Buddhism is over 2500 years old with over 400 million followers. It is one of the four biggest religions in the world. What do you think accounts for its success?

4. What do you think are the three most important things you have learned about Buddhism? Give three important values of your own as well. How do they compare?

5. List three or more of the hard things about being a Buddhist in Britain today. Explain your choices.

6. Buddhists seek to become 'enlightened', to see the light. How do you think Buddhism helps people to find 'the light'? What sort of 'light' is it?

7. 'To stop suffering you must stop desiring things' say Buddhists. What do they mean? If you were asked how to end suffering what would you say? Give three or more reasons to explain your answer.

8. 'Eight steps on the Noble Eightfold Path and eight spokes on the wheel of Dharma' is an explanation of Buddhism's common symbol. In what ways does Buddhism say life is like a wheel or like a path? What would you say your life is like – create a symbol for yourself.

9. If you could ask the Buddha five questions, what would they be and why?

10. Buddhists don't think that God can help you find the path for true living – everyone must find their own path. What do you think is the way to find the path to true living and why?

11. To be a good Buddhist, you must be harmless, and live without killing or causing others to kill. What would change if everyone in the world did this? Is it a good idea or not?

12. If you became a Buddhist, what would be good and what would be hard for you? (Don't do this question if you are a Buddhist; try question 16 instead.)

13. Buddhists think Siddhartha Gautama is one of the top leaders ever. What made him so brilliant at what he did?

14. Buddhists say they get strength, direction and purpose from the Noble Eightfold Path. How? What do you get direction from? Where does your sense of purpose come from?

15. What is respect and why is it important? What do Buddhists respect and how do they show that respect? What do you respect and how do you show it? What is similar and what is different between you and a Buddhist?

16. If you are a Buddhist make a list of the differences between what you learned in RE and what you learned from your family or the Sangha you go to.

Using Assessment Criteria to Boost Attainment

Assessing the outcomes of your work

Use this set of 'I can...' statements to help decide how well you have done in this unit's work. The emphasis is on 'learning from' Buddhism (AT2).

Draft your comments on the statement or statements you have chosen to write about. Talk about them with a partner in the class (and you talk about theirs) – use these levels to suggest ways in which each can improve your work.

Re-draft your answers and then hand it in to your teacher with a short statement about which level you think you have achieved and why. Remember you only need to achieve some of the statements to reach the appropriate level.

You can work at Level 3 if you can say 'yes' to most of these:	**I can ...** • say what I think about some Buddhist ways of doing things; • describe some Buddhist ideas simply; • talk about some of my questions about Buddhism; • make some links between my life and Buddhist life.
You can work at Level 4 if you can say 'yes' to most of these:	**I can ...** • suggest answers to the questions from my own experience; • make some sense of the life of the Buddha; • state my view on some puzzling questions about Buddhism; • refer to some teachings of Buddhism in describing my opinions; • say what Buddhists value, what I value, and why.
You can work at Level 5 if you can say 'yes' to most of these:	**I can ...** • explain what's most important to Buddhists, and to me; • respond to Buddhist ideas and teachings for myself; • give a well-informed reaction to Buddhist values; • give an explanation of Buddhist experience in an informed way; • relate my own view of the question to what Buddhists think and believe, expressing my views clearly and thoughtfully.
You can work at Level 6 if you can say 'yes' to most of these:	**I can ...** • express an insight into how and why Buddhists are inspired by the Buddha; • relate to the Buddhist idea of a leader and explain my own ideas about leadership clearly; • express my insights into what it's like to be a Buddhist in ways that connect up with my own life; • interpret Buddhist perspectives on values and what matters most; • express an insight of my own into some similarities and differences between Buddhism and another religion or way of life.

© 2006 RE Today Services
Permission is granted to photocopy this page for use in classroom activities in schools that have purchased this publication.

Teachings of Jesus: The Parable of the Sheep and the Goats

For information

The activities in this section use the parable of the Sheep and the Goats (Matthew 25: 31–46) to explore the concept of **judgement** within Christianity. This is a less well-known parable in today's Western culture because its focus is on the judgement of the individual (and group) for sins of both commission (bad deeds/actions done) and omission (good deeds/actions not done), something not 'popular' in contemporary culture. It is about the **final judgement of the whole universe at the end of all time**. God appears as a **judge** and also a **king**. God's kingdom offers **eternal life** to those who have been good and **eternal punishment** to those who have not. God will judge people according to their actions on earth: if they have helped others, then they have helped God. In the gospels, Jesus is seen as a **mediator** between God and humanity.

I can ...

Level 3
talk about how Jesus' teaching about what God is like affects how Christians live their lives;

make links between my life and how Christians might live their lives.

Level 4
show understanding of how artist(s) show the meaning of the parable in pictures to do with the Last Judgement;

apply my own ideas about the Last Judgement to talk about which painting I think is best.

Level 5
describe Christian views about judgement using biblical text to support my answers;

explain what I think about this parable and why it is challenging for some Christians.

For the teacher

A starter activity: Using no more than 60 words, identify the key points in the Parable of the Sheep and the Goats – this focuses pupils' attention on the key meaning and helps them engage with the biblical text.

Development: Read the 'Interpretations' and complete the tasks on page 13. This will enable pupils to engage with text at a deeper level, and use skills of interpretation, reflection and analysis.

Links

Themes: beliefs and concepts: some key ideas about Christian beliefs about judgement; **ethics and relationships:** exploring questions to do with right and wrong, actions and consequences.

Experiences and opportunities: pupils will discuss, question and evaluate the key Christian concept of judgement and reflect on its implication for action in the world today.

Using the stimulus sheet on page 14, pupils are required to think of the teachings in the Parable of the Sheep and the Goats in relationship to contemporary life, developing their skills of investigation and application.

Plenary: Return to the key summary points written to identify the key points of the parable. Reduce these to just two sentences.

Assessment task: The assessment task on page 15 uses both textual and creative responses to assess pupils' conceptual understanding as well as their reflection and response. The teacher will need to ensure that there is a supply of charcoal, coloured chalks, old magazines and newspapers, glue, brushes and paper available for those who choose to do the art-focused task. It would be good but not essential to have gathered together a number of different images of the Last Judgement to act as stimulus. The tasks are designed to appeal to a number of different learning styles. After the first task is completed, discuss the work with the pupils and feed back, identifying the level they have achieved so far, indicating what they must do in the subsequent questions to improve. The use of this 'assessment for learning' technique has been shown to have a powerful impact on motivation and progress.

Teachings of Jesus: The Parable of the Sheep and the Goats

> I think the parable means that God only loves good people. But I think if he only lets really good people into heaven then there mustn't be much room there.

> I always thought that Jesus taught people to forgive someone when they did something wrong. But in this story God doesn't forgive! This makes believing in the Bible very difficult for me – I am very confused.

> This is an absolute load of rubbish. Someone very sick has made this up to make everyone feel bad and to make them do what they want.

> I don't see why they have to use sheep and goats in the story. They are only dumb animals and could not possibly be responsible if they do right or wrong – so how come we use them to symbolise good and bad people?

Interpretations:

Jesus' Parable of the Sheep and the Goats

Matthew chapter 25 verses 31 to 46

> It's about time we all took notice of this story. Just think how much better the world would be if people stopped doing things just for themselves and looked after others more. There would be no crime, no wars, no starving, no homeless. What a brilliant place to live.

> It must be very difficult for Christians to try to be good all the time to stop them from being sent to hell. Who would want to believe in a God who is so strict?

> I think the message in this story is really what life is all about. We have to try to help other people all the time. The story tries to emphasise that this is what God really wants from us by saying he will judge us by how we have helped people in our lives.

> This story is scary. I mean, how can I be good all the time? Now I will worry that I will end up in hell.

- Discuss these 'interpretations' of the parable.
- Which **three** interpretations do you feel best sum up the key points of this parable?
- Which do you agree with?
- Which statements might have been said by an agnostic, by an atheist, or by a Christian who interprets the Bible literally?
- What does this parable say about God? Why do you think some Christians feel uncomfortable with this parable?

Engaging with secondary RE: Assessed RE

A research task....

- Look at the following statements from Jesus' parable about the Sheep and the Goats.

- In the parable, Jesus used 'sheep' to represent people who had done 'good' things and 'goats' to represent people who had either done bad things or not done good things.

- Using the same analogy, complete the table below, using examples you find in the media or from your own ideas and experiences.

Statement from parable	A 'sheep' today An example I have found…	A 'goat' today An example I have found…
I was hungry and you fed me		
I was thirsty and you gave me a drink		
I was a stranger and you welcomed me		
I was naked and you clothed me		
I was sick and you took care of me		
I was in prison and you visited me		

Teachings of Jesus: The Parable of the Sheep and the Goats

An assessment task: The Last Judgement

Your tasks...

1. **Imagine** you are present at the Last Judgement as told in the parable. Write **3 sentences** about each of the following:

a. What you **see**

b. What you **smell**

c. What you **hear**

d. What you **touch** (feel)

e. What you **taste**

f. How you are **feeling**

Either:

2. There is a lot of artwork based on the Last Judgement (for example Michelangelo did a section in the Sistine Chapel, as well as artists such as Bosch, Pieter Pourbus and Jan Paulus Maly). Some used the analogy of the sheep and the goats: others didn't. You are now going to **create** your own piece entitled either '**The Last Judgement**', '**Judging what is right and wrong**' or '**Who is the judge?**'. To do this you will need to draw on your understanding of the Parable of the Sheep and the Goats and your own thoughts about sin, right and wrong and God's judgement. To create your artwork you have a choice from charcoal, coloured chalks or images cut or torn from magazines and newspapers.

Or:

3. Some Christians find the parable of the Sheep and the Goats difficult. Why do you think this is?

Write 100–150 words to explore this idea, drawing on what the Bible says to support your answer. You might like to compare and contrast Matthew chapter 18 verses 10-14 with Matthew chapter 25 verses 31-46 or find some other suitable material to help.

Do you think there will be a 'Last Judgement'? Why? Why not? Write a further 70–100 words to explain your thinking.

© 2006 RE Today Services
Permission is granted to photocopy this page for use in classroom activities in schools that have purchased this publication.

Learning from Sikhism: Using a Question Bank

For the teacher

Learning from religion is often well facilitated by sharp questions at the end of a unit of teaching. A **'question bank'** approach provides a flexible structure for open-ended and self-differentiating work.

Pupils work in pairs to provide short reponses to three or four questions, selected from a larger number (page 17 provides 16; mostly you will want to work with a fewer number than this, probably 8 to 10). The activity is set up to incorporate peer assessment.

Learning objectives:

- **to reflect on** the relationship between beliefs, teachings and ultimate questions, communicating their own ideas using reasoned arguments;

- **to express insights** into the impact of religious belief on everyday life.

The activity works best when:

- **pupils:**
  - have opportunity to discuss the questions;
  - are familiar with using 'I can' statements and the process of peer assessment;
  - have some experience of writing to a given number of words.

- **the teacher:**
  - has selected or adapted questions from the question bank so that they are targeted and appropriate to the ability and learning needs of the class (as reflected in the examples of pupils' work on page 19);
  - has developed the 'I can' statements to relate specifically to the chosen questions (and the requirements of the syllabus being followed) and has shared them with pupils at the outset;
  - supports an 'open book' approach, where the emphasis is not on memorisation but on responding to substantive questions that require thinking and reasoning.

Links

Themes: beliefs and concepts: some key ideas, questions of meaning and beliefs in Sikhism.

Experiences and opportunities: pupils will be well prepared for this assessment activity if they have had opportunities to meet and talk.

Resources

Web

- Using digital video to support peer assessment in RE, an activity on Becta ICT Advice (choose 'Secondary' and 'RE').
  www.ictadvice.org.uk

Assessment activity 2:
Learning from Sikhism – using a question bank

For the teacher
Select from the questions, adapting and adding your own (as required by the details of your teaching and learning objectives and the needs and abilities of your pupils). Produce a **stimulus sheet** with the questions and the activity (below) clearly explained. **Open-ended questions** that require **thought, reasoning** and **response** are the order of the day.

 These questions are available for subscribers to download in Word format from www.retoday.org.uk

1. What do you think are the best things about being a young Sikh in Britain today? Why?	2. List three or more of the hard things about being a Sikh in Britain today. Explain why you chose these three.
3. If you could ask one of the gurus 5 questions, which guru would you interview, and what would you ask? Say why.	4. Many Sikhs think Guru Nanak is one of the top leaders ever. What made him so brilliant at what he did? What makes a great leader?
5. Make a list of what similarities and differences between one of the gurus and another inspiring human being (of your choice) you can see. Explain your list.	6. In Sikh families, being a follower of the path of the True Name matters. How do you think Sikhism helps people to find 'the true path in life'? What sort of path do you think this is?
7. Sikhs think that God can help you find the path for true living – everyone can know God for themselves, and follow God's way. What do you think is the way to find the path for true living?	8. One Sikh mum says, 'I get strength, directions and purposes from the Rehat Maryada' (the Sikh code of Good Living). How do you think this happens? What do you get direction from? Where does your sense of purpose come from?
9. Sikhism is over 500 years old, and has over 22 million followers. It is one of six main religions in the UK. What do you think accounts for its success?	10. 'To be a good Sikh, you must be devoted to God, generous and willing to serve others. You must not discriminate against people for their sex, race, age or any other cause… You must not fear, or frighten.' What would change if everyone in the world did this? Is it a good idea?
11. 'God is not a Hindu or a Muslim' said the guru. What did he mean? If you were asked how to talk about God what would you say? Give at least three reasons to explain your answer	12. What is respect, and why is it important? List some ways of showing respect that you know Sikhs use to show respect for the Guru Granth Sahib, treated as a human guru. What do Sikhs respect? What do you respect? How do you show it?
13. Values: from your study, give three things that matter to Sikhs – say why. Then give three important values of your own as well. How do yours compare with the Sikh values?	14. If you became a Sikh, what would be good and what would be hard for you? (Don't do this question if you are a Sikh: try Question 15 instead.)
15. If you are a Sikh, make a list of the differences between what you learned in RE and what you learned from the family or the gurudwara about your faith this year.	16. 'We treat the Guru Granth Sahib as a living guru. This is symbolic, but it's more than that – these words are, for us, the way to God.' Explain how Sikhs revere their scriptures, and give your respectful reactions to these practices.

Activity for pupils
Choose four questions from the question bank and **discuss** them with a partner. **Write** 75 words in answer to each of the four you choose. When you have written your answer, **peer-mark** with a partner, using the list of 'I can …' statements. What level do you think you got and why?

Digital video ... supporting peer assessment
Ideas for adapting this work

Digital video (DV) is a classroom tool that can be powerfully used to support peer assessment in RE. It provides an **alternative method** for pupils to **record understanding** and is more suited to some pupils' preferred learning style, e.g. visual/spatial, bodily/kinaesthetic.

How one RE teacher used DV in this context is outlined on the Becta ICT Advice website (see 'Resources').

In the lesson pupils:

- **prepared** their presentation in note form
- **practised** and recorded their key points
- **talked** about ways they could improve
- **watched** a playback of two of the recordings – and **fed back** positively to presenters.

Learning from religion: I can ...

You can work at **Level 3** if you can say 'yes' to most of these:	• *say what I think about some Sikh ways of doing things* • *ask good questions of my own about some aspects of being a Sikh* • *suggest some things that influence Sikhs, and some things that influence me* • *make some links between my life and Sikh life*
You can work at **Level 4** if you can say 'yes' to most of these:	• *suggest answers to questions about Sikhs from my own experience* • *make some sense of the life of the gurus* • *give my view on some puzzling questions about Sikhism* • *refer to the teaching of Sikhism in explaining my opinions* • *say what Sikhs value, and why*
You can work at **Level 5** if you can say 'yes' to most of these:	• *explain what's most important to Sikhs, and to me* • *respond thoughtfully to information about Sikh teaching for myself.* • *give an informed reaction to some Sikh values* • *respond to what Sikhs experience in an informed way* • *relate my own view of a question to what Sikhs think and believe*
You can work at **Level 6** if you can say 'yes' to most of these:	• *express my insight into how and why Sikhs are inspired by the gurus* • *relate to the Sikh idea of a leader and explain my own idea clearly* • *consider the challenges of what a Sikh might say about God, and express my own insights into the question* • *evaluate a Sikh perspective on values and what matters most* • *relate my own views of life to Sikh teaching and ideas*
You can work at **Level 7** if you can say 'yes' to most of these:	• *evaluate what Sikhs say about the life story of Guru Nanak* • *use evidence and examples to explain clearly and in detail what I think about key aspects of Sikhism, as compared with another religion* • *express with examples what Sikhs are committed to, and what I am committed to* • *evaluate Sikh ideas about life's meaning and purpose with evidence and examples, in relation to my own ideas and another religion*

Learning from Sikhism – Using a Question Bank

Responses from pupils

Sikhism: Learning from the religion

Sikh means disciple. What kind of person would you follow? Highlight the qualities they would have?

The kind of person I would follow is a person who is serious about their religion. Also, would try to set and example, so people could follow it. The person would help people in need, and his qualities would be honesty, because people who follow a person, always need the truth. Another quality is modesty because the person who is being followed should thank the people who believe in him, not get carried away. Other qualities are:- kindness, truthfulness, clean and caring.

Sikhs say that they get strength from the Guru Granth Sahib. How? What do you get strength from?

Sikhs get strength from Guru Granth Sahib because they are reading the teachings of the people, they couldn't meet. So they know what and what not to do. I get my strength for Quran, the holy book of Islam. As the same as Sikhs I am reading the teachings of my religion.

Sikhs believe in one God only. What do you believe about God?

I also believe that there is one God and also that he has no son or daughter. I believe that he is the master of the universe and no one can better him. I believe God created everything and everyone. I believe God can do anything.

Attif is in year 8. He has tackled questions 4, 8 and 11 (from the question bank). He has made some appropriate links with his own experience. However, he tends to state information rather than provide reasoned comments and evidence of reflection.

Sikhism

If I could chose my leader I would make sure that he was brave by seeing if he would sacrifice his life for his people, but I wouldn't let him die until necessary though. He would need to be fair and treat inferior as equals and be selfless in the way that he doesn't think of himself.

I believe that there is one God and that Jesus was a messenger. I think of God as a man up in heaven. Trying to prevent death and poverty and return it with happiness and good will. Comic relief must be like christmas for him. People should help and encourage their friends.

If everyone was charitable to the poor the rich would become poor and the poor would be rich. The poor might take advantage of the publics generosity. People would take money and generosity for granted. It is not a good or bad idea but should be exercised with caution.

If I could wear symbols on my clothing it would be all the religious symbols and pictures of gods to show that I treat all religions with equality. I would also have famous phrases from religious scriptures printed on.

Sam is in year 8. He has tackled questions 4, 11 and 10 (from the question bank) and has achieved level 6. His RE teacher commented that this was his best work all year, thoughtful, speculative and responding to what has been taught rather than just announcing his opinions.

Assessing Skills and Viewpoints: Beliefs About God

For the teacher

Skills not stance: This piece of work uses atheism and agnosticism as a stimulus to good learning and assessment. Some teachers find the presence of atheist views and agnostic stances awkward in RE, but controversy is the life blood of the subject, and the 'level 8 atheist' is a fine product of quality RE. There are too many level 1 atheists in class: they say 'God – well, s'obvious innit? There ain't one.' Teacher asks why, and they display their philosophical depth: 'Dunno.' But level 8 atheists can argue coherently and in a well-informed and multi-disciplinary fashion that God is not real. They are good at RE.

Web Links
www.pcfre.org.uk/spiritedarts
www.pcfre.org.uk/db
(for moderated database)

These two areas of the Professional Council for RE's website offer great opportunities for interactive work around diverse views about God and showcase some marvellous creative ideas and the diverse views of thousands of young people. Set pupils a homework task to research what 30 atheists, agnostics and non-religious people think about God, from the

Links to QCA's RE Schemes of Work
This work connects to the QCA's Framework and Scheme of Work by enabling learners to consider beliefs and concepts, to learn from non-religious views of life, and to develop skills of dialogue and argument.

Resource
BBC Curriculum Bites RE Series 2 ISBN 1-904024-70-X *'Is God Real?'* Available from RE Today, very good for this topic.

Assessment stems for pupils to use: 'I can...'

Level 3
describe some beliefs about God.

say what I think about questions to do with belief in God.

Level 4
show that I understand two points of view about God.

apply the ideas of atheists or agnostics to what I think about God.

Level 5
explain three different ideas about the question 'Is God real?' for myself.

express my view of three arguments about God, using correct religious vocabulary.

Level 6
interpret the reasons why different people hold their views on atheism or theism.

express my own insight into arguments and experiences that lead people to their answers to 'God questions'.

Assessment task: Argument and reflection

Sometimes there seems to be a conflict between the 'argumentative atheist' and the 'touchy feely spiritual' believer in God. In real life, atheists and believers in God both hold to their views because of reasons and experiences.

How to run this assessment task

Use the **three statements of different viewpoints** on page 21 for discussion with pupils. Ask them to highlight what they agree and disagree with in each.

Use the **examples of work** on page 22 to show pupils what level 4 and level 5 look like. Good models inspire success!

Use the **multi-choice writing frame** on page 23 to guide pupils to write well. There are many different ways to approach it, so it is self-differentiating. You will be surprised by the quality this simple writing strategy produces.

Assessing Skills and Viewpoints: Beliefs About God

Atheist, Agnostic, Theist:
three viewpoints with arguments and experience

My name is Athelia Atheist.
Here's why I'm an atheist. Although millions of people believe in God, they could all be wrong. Prayers don't stop people from suffering and dying, and worship doesn't make you nice – some religious people preach about love, but seem full of hate to me. They often say 'God' explains where we came from, but if so, where did this 'God' come from? They all think their holy books are true, but I've read some of the Bible and the Gita and they read like old fables to me. They think that when you die, there is heaven or nirvana, but I think it looks most likely that we just lie in the grave. The clincher for me is all the evil in the world. Just look at it – cancer, tsunamis, child abuse. How could there be a God in charge of a world like this?

My name is Ann Agnostic.
I don't think anyone can be sure about God really. People mean lots of different things by the word 'God'. Some say it's a 'he' but why not a female God? Some people say they hear God's voice, but some of them are psychotic, and do evil in God's name. I've tried praying, and sometimes you get a feeling that someone might be listening, sometimes even an answer to the prayer. But then why so many unanswered prayers? Ambiguity – it means that the evidence points in both directions at once – is the normal feeling I get about God. I think you could only be sure of God after death – and perhaps then we will just be nothing, so we'll never know. I don't mind being agnostic. It's interesting, and I think it's the only sensible viewpoint in the end.

I'm called Theo Theist.
I believe in God, and here's why. When I was a tiny baby, I nearly died, but my whole family and people at my church prayed 'round the clock' for me. The doctors were amazed that I lived, but here I am. I thank God for my life. And I'm not a believer in God just because of this. I also know that God's presence can be felt. Sometimes I feel this when I go to worship or pray, or when I'm climbing (I do rock climbing). My explanation for all the beauty in the world and all the love is that our universe began with God. My idea is that God is eternal, so has no beginning, but all created things come from God. This isn't to say that I never have doubts – there is pain in the world as well as goodness. But in the end, I find it makes sense of my life to trust in God, so I do.

© 2006 RE Today Services
Permission is granted to photocopy this page for use in classroom activities in schools that have purchased this publication.

Examples of pupils' work about beliefs

The task, set as homework, was to create a page that expressed your own beliefs. In this piece of work, George shows that he is able to work at level 4. He can apply ideas about belief from his studies to his own point of view. Next, he needs to show that he understands different religious beliefs by referring to them in detail.

In this part of her piece of work, Charlotte shows that she is able to work at level 5. Answering a 'mysterious question' about the purpose of our lives, she uses concepts of humanism, atheism and the idea of a righteous life to express her own views clearly about questions of meaning and purpose. Next she needs to consider how to interpret the ideas of 'theory' 'evidence' and 'proof' in relation to questions about religion.

I think we choose are own purpose in life just like the humanist think. I think this because not every body is the same. not everybody does the same things and not everybody enjoys the same activities, so really it would be very hard for us all to have the same purpose in life. I think we are here to live and enjoy our life following Gods way. In my life I try to follow a rightous life but I also try to enjoy life. I don't agree with the athests point of view that we were here by accident I believe somthing had to have put us here. I'm not sure about the evolution theory because all the scientific evidence supports the theory but also someone must of put the monkeys on the earth.

Assessing Skills and Viewpoints: Beliefs About God

My beliefs about God: a multi-choice writing frame

Instructions for pupils: In this assessment, you are going to write about **your own beliefs**. Good work will relate your beliefs to those of others thoughtfully. Do your best. Look at the prompts in the nine boxes below, and highlight at least twelve of them, including at least one from each box, that you want to write about. You can cross the others out. Use the prompts to draft your 'essay', then swap it with a partner, and each mark the other person's work. Rewrite the essay to include all the improvements your partner suggests.

Beginnings...	**Issues...**	**Christians think...**
• In this essay... • The question I'm thinking and writing about is... • What's interesting about this topic is... • There are many different ideas about... • Questions about God are hard to answer because...	• If God made everything, then who made God?' What I think about this is... • There are 6 billion people in the world. About 4 per cent are atheists. This makes me think... • Suffering and evil are a problem for believers in a good God...	• Christians believe God came to earth as Jesus. It seems to me... • Christians think God will meet us when we die... • Christians explain the beginning of the universe by referring to the love of God... • Christians believe God is full of love...
Atheists argue...	**Sikhs believe...**	**Agnostics aren't sure...**
• Atheists believe there's no God. I think... • If God is not real, then... • You can't prove atheism, but... • How can there be a God when there's so much...	• Guru Nanak had a vision of God. I think... • Nanak taught that God can be known through serving other people. I think... • Nanak believed God is the source of beauty. My view is...	• There's no proof about God, so... • Evidence for God is mixed... • If God is real, then why... • If there's no God, then how... • 'God questions' are hard to answer because... • You can't ever be sure about God because...
It makes you think...	**What I believe...**	**Conclusions...**
• When people say 'God' they mean... • If there's no God, then... • There must be a God because... • There can't be a God because...	• I believe... • I have always wondered... • Someone I respect says... • The main idea I believe is... • A person who influenced me... • I'm still thinking about...	• This essay has been interesting because... • My conclusions are... • It's important to remember... • There is no proof about... • My answer to the question is...

© 2006 RE Today Services
Permission is granted to photocopy this page for use in classroom activities in schools that have purchased this publication.

Learning and Assessment: Islam and the Idea of God

For the teacher

This range of strategies enables pupils to think about the Islamic understanding of God. The activities are suitable for pupils aged 14–15, including those studying this topic for GCSE or standard grade religious studies examinations. The assessment activity (page 27) enables pupils to express their responses to the work undertaken. The beliefs are illustrated with quotations from Muslim young people, with the first Surah of the Qur'an and with a stunning artistic image of the 99 names of Allah.

An English rendering of the First Surah of the Holy Qur'an

In the name of Allah, the beneficent, the merciful

Praise be to Allah, Lord of the worlds

Ruler of the day of Judgement

You alone we worship, you alone we ask for help

Show us the straight path: the path of those who you have favoured

Not the path of those who anger you

Not the path of those who go astray.

Learning objectives

This set of classroom activities are designed to enable pupils to:

- **describe** some Muslim beliefs about Allah, using simple Muslim vocabulary (L3)
- **show** that they **understand** what **impact** Islamic theology has on believers (L4)
- **apply** the idea of faith to some of their own behaviour (L4)
- **explain** three different ways in which belief in Allah has an **impact** on young Muslims' lives (L5)
- **express** their own ideas about belief in God in the light of Islamic and Qur'anic understanding (L5)
- **interpret** the Islamic idea of Allah in relation to another view of God (L6).

For information

On the back cover of this resource, we reproduce, by kind permission, Ahmed Moustapha's excellent image 'The Attributes of Divine Perfection'. This image is used here to support and develop pupils' understanding of Muslim concepts of God. It incorporates 99 geometric shapes, each written with on of the beautiful names of Allah, thus, following Islamic convention, expressing an Islamic understanding of the divine without making an image.

Learning and Assessment: Islam and the Idea of God

Activity 1
Working with Muslim young people's insight

Copy a set of the twelve cards on page 26 for each trio of pupils. Cut them up and put the twelve cards into an envelope. Ask the three to take four cards each, and consider what they show about Muslim belief. All the ideas on the cards are authentic British Muslim young people's reflections on belief in Allah, the first pillar of the faith. For the school with few Muslim pupils, they enable a simple encounter with authentic young Muslims' perspectives. All these are taken from the Professional Council for RE's moderated database of young people's writing about religious and spiritual questions. Many more can be found at www.pcfre.org.uk/db. It is possible to use these cards in a variety of ways. For example, ask groups to:

- **rank** the statements from 'most insightful' to 'least insightful'.
- **match** the statements on the cards to aspects of the first Surah of the holy Qur'an (see page 24 for English rendition).
- **write** two questions they would like to ask each of the speakers from the cards. How might the Muslim young people reply?
- **write** their own statement about God – they can then submit these to the website if they wish.

These activities will contribute to the assessment task (page 27), so following good practice it would be good to show pupils the end task, and have it discussed in pairs along the way.

Activity 2
Whispering angels and demons

In the same trios, ask pupils to prepare a short debate about God. It can be rehearsed but should be unscripted. 'Whispering angel / whispering demon' is an excellent, flexible strategy for well-targeted classroom talk. One of the key beliefs of Islam is that God is most great. His angels are guides for humanity, but Iblis, the Shaytan, is a fallen angel who whispers deceit and temptation to the believer. In this 'talk and listen' learning strategy, one pupil is a listener. One takes the role of the deceiver, and suggests as many reasons as possible why the listener should not believe in God's great power. The third takes the role of an angel, and whispers all the reasons for belief in divine power. Although the idea borrows from Islamic theology, it really provides for the development of young people's own ideas about God. It is challenging and powerfully empathic if pupils take the role opposite to their own beliefs.

Engaging with secondary RE: Assessed RE

I believe there is only one God – Allah. God watches all we do and is always there to help and guide us. I follow Islam: you should pray five times a day to thank God for everything he has given you, to ask for forgiveness in anything you've done wrong. Everyone should be treated equally. It is not right to criticise people that God has made. I have learnt to keep to what I am allowed or not allowed to do. I have learnt to forgive, whatever the situation.

Girl, 15

I believe in ONE God, this is because to everything in life there is a limit, so on top of these limited factors there MUST be an UNLIMITED factor: this is God in English, Allah in Arabic. God sees the rules to life and is the almighty.

Boy, 14

I believe in the oneness of Allah. He has no partner, he has no son. He wasn't born, he does not give birth and there is nothing at all like him. He can do everything, anything. He can hear and see you wherever you are.

Girl, 11

My belief in God is very strong. God helps us through difficult paths in life; he is very loyal and is like an invisible friend to me. He is precious, and is a very important person in our lives.

Girl 15

I think God is ... well ... God, I guess. God is God, our creator, and He is very powerful. That all I can say. He is not something you can measure.

Girl, 15

I feel that Allah (God) is with me and wherever I am. I think Allah is the real God. No one can see him but he can see us. He is one, he has no partner and he wasn't born. When you pray you feel closer to God. You are thanking him for what you have got. I think religion completes your life. Without it you can get lost and confused.

Boy, 11

To be honest there is no one who can describe God because God is invisible. God is powerful in every way. My own thoughts about God are that you should always think that God exists and always believe in God and be happy that God is always there.

Girl, 15

I think God exists. In my religion we cannot think of a creation for him. He created everything, he is everywhere, he can do anything and he has all powers. I can only describe him by his names.

Boy, 14

I believe in one God, ALLAH. I don't know what my God looks like because in the Muslim religion we are not allowed to see any pictures of 'him'. As a Muslim I think Allah is the most powerful 'thing' as I don't know what 'he' is like. I respect my God very much.

Girl, 14

I am a Muslim so my beliefs about God are fairly orthodox. I believe God is an entity which is beyond the scope of human perception (which is pretty limited to say the least...). God is within all of us, He is the voice which guides us down the path of goodness. The Hand of God is on all of us – it's our choice whether to take it or not.

Boy, 15

I believe in God a lot. I believe that God is kind and generous. God made this world full of joy, or if he was cruel, he would have made the world unhappy and sad not joyful. GOD IS FULL OF JOY!

Girl, 11

I think that another human couldn't have created all the humans in the world so I believe the only alternative is that Allah did it and that He is so great that He was able to create every fibre and every cell in the human body. How many human bodies are there in the world? Who created the earth and everything in it? Allah, because there can't have coincidentally been a big bang to create planets, could there? Also I believe that not even a leaf falls or a snow flake drops without it being the will of Allah.

Boy 13

Assessment: Complete these questions from the work we have done. Aim for the highest level of skill you can.

What have you learned about Islam and Allah?

Use your *knowledge* and *understanding* to answer fully.

1. Describe what Muslims believe about Allah.
2. Choose three words from the list below, and say your understanding of how a Muslim uses these words:
   - Allah
   - Beneficent
   - All Powerful
   - Revelation
   - Lord of the Worlds
   - Ruler of the Day of Judgement
   - 99 Names
3. Imagine a Muslim meets an atheist: 'You believe something impossible...' How does the conversation continue?
4. Choose *at least two* of these quotations, and give your own understanding or interpretation.
   - 'Allah is one, and besides him there is no other.'
   - 'Allah is the ruler of the day of Judgement.'
   - 'The Christians, Muslims, Sikhs and Jews all worship one God. Is it the same God?'
   - 'Any image or picture you made of God would be a lie.'
   - 'When we go walking towards God, then God comes running towards us.'
   - 'In the creation of heaven and earth and the difference between night and day, Allah has hidden signs of his sovereignty.'
5. What did you learn about young Muslims from our work on what they said?

What have you learned from Islam about Allah and theism?

Use your *reflections* and *personal* ideas to be as *insightful* as you can.

1. Are you an atheist, an agnostic or a theist? Why? Is there anything that might change your current thinking? What? Why? Why not?
2. There are about 1 200 000 000 (1.2 billion) Muslims in the world. Is their shared experience and belief evidence that Allah is real?
3. Muslims say all images of God are misleading. Can you think of one misleading image of God, perhaps that you used to believe in but don't now? Are all images of God misleading or not?
4. Where is God? Muslims say Allah can be seen in the creation, heard in the words of the Qur'an and felt in the human heart. What do you think of claims to see, hear or feel God?
5. Muslims have 99 names for Allah. These include: Judge / Sovereign / Almighty / Evolver / Revealer / Guardian / Masterful / Compassionate / Oft-forgiving, and ninety others. Choose five words you would use to describe God. Write a sentence or two to say why you chose each one.

I can ...

- describe what Muslims believe about God and *make links with how their belief affects their life. I can talk about my own beliefs about God and if that affects my life*. (L3)
- show understanding of how Muslim belief about God is expressed through their religious practices and *describe how this belief inspires them. I can describe who or what inspires me in my life*. (L4)
- suggest how and why Muslim belief about God is different from and/or similar to at least one other religion and *explain what inspires and influences me taking into account these teachings about God*. (L5)
- give an informed account of Muslim belief about God *interpreting this in relation of another religion's and my own view about God*. (L5)

'More or Less' Task Setting

For information

Helping all achieve to their full potential in RE means having to cater for a range of abilities in every class, although the breadth of the range may be different in different classes and in different schools. Tasks need to be set to **support** and **challenge** the learning of all. This is at the heart of the process of **differentiation** which links implicitly with developing a **personalised learning** RE curriculum focused on the needs of all. If tasks are set at a level that is not high enough for the more able, or at a level where the less able cannot access them, then pupils will become de-motivated and will disengage from their learning and consequently not achieve the **standards** which they are capable.

For the teacher : Focusing on the 'less able'

It is important to recognise the particular 'special' needs of pupils across lower secondary (KS3) in mainstream schools. This could include those who have significant difficulties in learning, those with disabilities which may impede their learning and those who have difficulties with reading and/or writing, but not with being able to grapple with religious concepts and understanding. Look at your lesson planning and resources, bearing the needs of the less able in mind and ask yourself:

As a department do we:

- take account of the emotional and social maturity of less able pupils, recognising that resources that are too childish humiliate and de-motivate them?

- ensure that pupils with literacy difficulties are given suitable texts? Are our stimulus and worksheets clearly presented? Do we have simple writing frames, provide sentence starters and help them with 'reading clues' by using standard, reasonably sized text, a clear font, good line spacing, simple language, fewer questions, larger spacing for writing, etc?

- have assessment tasks that do not always require individual written work? Can we develop assessment tasks for pairs and groups? How can we assess their contributions to discussions? Should we allow them to record their answers? Can we think of creative and ICT strategies that allow them to show what they can achieve?

- recognise that pupils quickly become de-motivated when they are not sure what is required: so have we broken down tasks into easily identifiable 'incremental goals'?

Activity: A task, differentiated for the less able

The main task is to write about 250 words on what pupils have discovered about Christian and scientific thought on the origins of the world, and compare these with their own views. Less able pupils might address the same question with the following series of structured sentence starters in a writing frame (select as appropriate):

- Christians believe that the world was created by...
- I agree/disagree with this because...
- Science tells us that the universe came into existence because...
- I agree/disagree with this because...
- The world is so beautiful that it could not have been made by accident. I agree/disagree with this because...
- God created the world but it took millions of years. I agree/disagree with this because...
- The world happened just by accident. I agree / disagree with this because...
- The main similarities between the views of a Christian and a scientist who does not believe in God about how the universe began are...
- The main differences between Christian and atheist views on how the universe began are...
- One question I would like to ask about how the universe began is...
- Another question I would like to ask is...

This example is taken from *Steps in RE: Onwards and Upwards* (ISBN 1-904024-86-6, RE Today 2006) which focuses on the additional support needs of pupils aged 11 to 14 (lower secondary/KS3) in mainstream schools.

'More or Less' Task Setting

For the teacher: Focusing on the 'more able'

Tasks set in RE can sometimes allow for a range of different responses that pupils of a range of abilities can access. Sometimes they do not. High-achieving pupils often need more **challenge** than can be afforded by the 'general task' which can sometimes impose an artificial ceiling on their achievement. This is something that needs to be taken into consideration when tasks are set, either for the class or for groups within a class. **'Extension tasks'** for the more able can sometimes be merely 'more of the same' whereas they should be **extending** and **challenging** the **learning**. If the 'extension task' really is doing that then isn't it the sort of task that the most able should be doing from the beginning of their work time rather than after they have completed the same task as everyone else?

The two examples below focus on differentiating tasks for the more able. The first looks at a task for 11–12-year-olds and the second looks at task and questions using higher-level skill words to bring about higher-level responses. All pupils, but especially the more able, often respond well when given a choice. The teacher's task is to ensure that questions and activities set are intriguing, that they stir curiosity and imagination and present them with a challenge.

Activity 1:
Differentiating for the most able: Learning from the Five Pillars of Islam

- Muhammad ﷺ asked Muslims to show their religion in five ways, something all the time, something daily, something when you're paid, something annually and something once in a lifetime.
- Draw up a writing frame (based on these five things) for pupils to record their reflections on their own pattern of life and intention, clarified by their study of five pillars in Islam (level 3 or 4).
- This task can be extended by asking pupils to write a longer piece (as a story, poem or reflection) on one of the five items from their writing frame. It can be assessed at level 5 or 6 providing that they are encouraged to illustrate distinctive beliefs and express their own views on the challenges of being Muslim (level 5) and interpret sources and arguments and express their own views on the values and commitments that underpin being a Muslim (level 6).

Activity 2
Differentiating for the most able: Focus on skill development

Task for the whole class	Task for the more able
Retell 2 parables of Jesus that deal with wealth and poverty (L2), and describe the dangers that Jesus warns rich people about. (L3)	Explain how these two parables show what Christians believe about God and how they provide answers to questions about how they should live. (L5)
Design an Eid card that shows you understand what the meaning of the celebration is for Muslims. (L4)	Explain clearly three similarities and three differences and the beliefs they represent between Eid and a festival such as Divali or Easter. (L5/6)
Describe three ways Hindus and Christians show respect at their places of worship. What do you respect and how do you show it? (L4)	Defend your view of whether sacred buildings should be exempt from Council Tax or not: is this a way for the whole society to show respect for worship? (L6)
'Christmas is a festival for everyone'. Describe three different ways of celebrating Christmas (Anglican, Orthodox and Secular). Explain who would choose each of these and why. (L5)	Give argument and examples to show why some people say 'Christmas is no longer a Christian festival' and others say 'Christmas is the gift of the Christians to the whole community'. (L7)

Engaging with secondary RE: Assessed RE

Peer and Self-Assessment in RE

For information

Using peer and self-assessment enables pupils to take **responsibility** for their learning. Used well, this can raise their self-esteem and motivation and hence overall improvement. In any kind of assessment activity or task, clearly defined and pupil-friendly **learning objectives** are essential in order for pupils to understand what is expected of them. **Peer assessment** gives pupils the opportunity to talk about what they have learned, to recognise their achievements and evaluate what they must do to improve, based on interaction with their peers. Most pupils find this both engaging and useful and they quickly develop honest and reflective ways of responding to each other. **Self-assessment** enables pupils to evaluate their own performance over a period, against set criteria. It encourages them to consider how they can improve their work in the future. When setting a peer assessment task or devising a self-assessment sheet, ensure that you ask the kind of questions that address how the pupils learn (metacognition) and that there are clear criteria against which they can match their performance. An example of a peer assessment task and of a self-assessment approach is provided here for use or adaptation.

For the teacher: A task including peer marking

Use PCfRE's moderated database (**www.pcfre.org.uk/db**) of young people's comments about their beliefs and thoughts on particular questions. Choose one question as applicable to your scheme of work. Set the following task:

- Choose two religions you have been studying and find out what the young people from those religions say about the chosen question as recorded on the database. Discuss the answers with a partner; then, individually, write a summary in no more than 150 words, identifying the main points, how the opinions differ and if all members of one religion say the same thing (saying why and why not).

- In the light of what the young people say, explain your own views on the question (150 words max.).

Groups/pairs mark the work using a range of levels which have been written specifically for the task as 'I can …' statements (examples given on this page). Each group/pair discuss why a piece of work should be given a particular level and what needs to be done by each pupil to improve their work further and perhaps even 'go up' a level.

Take a different question and repeat the task.

Groups/pairs again mark the work, identifying the progress they have made.

I can…

Level 3	Level 4	Level 5	Level 6
• recognise some similarities and/or differences in the beliefs of two religions. • link my own beliefs to those two religions.	• describe key beliefs in two religions. • suggest answers to belief questions from my point of view, referring to religious teaching	• explain how key beliefs make a difference to individuals in two religions. • make an informed response to religious beliefs and commitments, explaining my own answers to religious questions.	• explain, showing knowledge and understanding, how beliefs in two religions are diverse and how they make a difference to people's lives • explain a range of religious perspectives relating them to my own and others' views.

Peer and Self Assessment in RE

Lower Secondary – Your self-assessment in Religious Education

Name ....

Class ....

Date ....

My target grade is ....

Look at these sentence starters:
1 I have done very well at...
2 I have done quite well at...
3 I need to do better at...
4 I need to do much better at...
5 I haven't had much of a chance as yet at...

1 Show, by circling the correct number, which sentence starter you would use in front of the statements below:

- 1 2 3 4 5 ... building up my factual knowledge of the religion(s) we are studying.
- 1 2 3 4 5 ... understanding and explaining 'why' questions in depth.
- 1 2 3 4 5 ... explaining links between religious beliefs and authorities and behaviour.
- 1 2 3 4 5 ... using sacred texts and quotes to support my work.
- 1 2 3 4 5 ... giving clear examples and arguments to go with my opinions.
- 1 2 3 4 5 ... explaining and using general concepts like 'worship', 'belief' and 'value'.
- 1 2 3 4 5 ... analysing similarities and differences between two religions I am studying.
- 1 2 3 4 5 ... interpreting the differences between groups within the religions.
- 1 2 3 4 5 ... using reasoning and examples to show I understand relationships between beliefs, teachings and world issues.
- 1 2 3 4 5 ... evaluating the significance of religious world views for life and living today.
- 1 2 3 4 5 ... keeping my work well organised and clear, including completing the basic notes I need for revision.
- 1 2 3 4 5 ... using lesson time and homework time effectively, including keeping up with my coursework responsibilities.

2. My comment on how much I have learned is ...

3. To improve further I need to ...

4. I would also like to say ...

© 2006 RE Today Services
Permission is granted to photocopy this page for use in classroom activities in schools that have purchased this publication.

Engaging with secondary RE: Assessed RE

Upper Secondary – Your self-assessment in Religious Education

Name ....

Class ....

Date ....

My target grade is ....

Look at these sentence starters:

1 I have done very well at...

2 I have done quite well at...

3 I need to do better at...

4 I need to do much better at...

5 I haven't had much of a chance as yet at...

1 Show, by circling the correct number, which sentence starter you would use in front of the statements below:

1 2 3 4 5 ... building up my factual knowledge of the religion(s) we are studying.

1 2 3 4 5 ... understanding and explaining 'why' questions in depth.

1 2 3 4 5 ... explaining links between religious beliefs and authorities and behaviour.

1 2 3 4 5 ... using sacred texts and quotes to support my work.

1 2 3 4 5 ... giving clear examples and arguments to go with my opinions.

1 2 3 4 5 ... explaining and using general concepts like 'worship', 'belief' and 'value'.

1 2 3 4 5 ... analysing similarities and differences between two religions I am studying.

1 2 3 4 5 ... interpreting the differences between groups within the religions.

1 2 3 4 5 ... using reasoning and examples to show I understand relationships between beliefs, teachings and world issues.

1 2 3 4 5 ... evaluating the significance of religious world views for life and living today.

1 2 3 4 5 ... keeping my work well organised and clear, including completing the basic notes I need for revision.

1 2 3 4 5 ... using lesson time and homework time effectively, including keeping up with my coursework responsibilities.

My progress since the last assessment has been ...

To keep on target for the grade I am aiming at I need to improve ...

The aspects of my work I am struggling with at the moment are ...

The aspects of my work which I am pleased with and encouraged by are ...